Porsche 356
1948 - 1965
Photo Album

Edited by Wallace A. Wyss
Preface by Kurt Oblinger
Foreword by Bob Holbert

Iconografix
Photo Album Series

Iconografix seeks collections of archival photographs for reproduction in future books. We require a minimum of 120 photographs per subject in our Photo Archive Series and Photo Album Series, and a minimum of 500 photographs per subject in our Photo Gallery Series. We prefer subjects narrow in focus, i.e., a specific model, or manufacturer, railroad, racing venue, etc. Photographs must be of high-quality, suited to reproduction in an 8x10-inch format. We willingly pay for the use of photographs.

If you own or know of such a collection, please contact: The Publisher, Iconografix, PO Box 446, Hudson, Wisconsin 54016 USA.

Iconografix
PO Box 446
Hudson, Wisconsin 54016 USA

Text Copyright © 1998

All rights reserved. No part of this work may be reproduced or used in any form by any means... graphic, electronic, or mechanical, including photocopying, recording, taping, or any other information storage and retrieval system... without written permission of the publisher.

We acknowledge that certain words, such as model names and designations, mentioned herein are the property of the trademark holder. We use them for purposes of identification only. This is not an official publication.

Iconografix books are offered at a discount when sold in quantity for promotional use. Businesses or organizations seeking details should write to the Marketing Department, Iconografix, at the above address.

Library of Congress Card Number 97-075280

ISBN 1-882256-85-9

98 99 00 01 02 03 04 5 4 3 2 1

Printed in the United States of America

PREFACE

The first time a Porsche 356 caught my eye was in high school in 1973. It was a pale yellow SC sunroof coupe owned by an attractive classmate. In retrospect, it's hard to remember whether I was more interested in the car or the girl. I took up photography after high school and was drawn to the color and motion of sports car racing. Even in the mid-1970s the 356s, particularly the Speedster, were contenders consistently beating much newer machinery. A race prepped Speedster always seemed to present such a pure form, nearly the perfect sports car.

In 1983 one of my photos was selected for the annual Porsche Racing Calendar as part of a worldwide contest. The contest prize was a trip to the Porsche factory and a tour of their other facilities. At the time the factory museum was a small building adjacent to the main factory. The first car you saw upon entering the hall was 356 number 1. Immediately across from it was the 956 that had just won LeMans. The relationship was symbolic of the part the 356 has played in Porsche's history, it was the beginning, the foundation upon which Porsche's formidable reputation was built. The last event on my tour agenda was the annual Porsche Cup awards banquet where the company celebrates its successes and honors the best Porsche privateer racers in the world. One of the honorees was Joe Cogbill, a veteran SCCA racer who had won a National Championship that year in a 356 that was nearly as old as myself.

Here in Southern California, 356s of every age are a common sight on the road. Some are show quality while others wear the dings and dents of use much like an old soldier displays his service ribbons. The fact that so many 356s are still in use is a tribute to the durable design and solid engineering of the car. Even now, 50 years on, the 356's styling is still attractive and pleasing. It can be said with certainty that it "just looks right".

I have never owned a 356 or any other Porsche for that matter. My personal collection is strongly English, but the 356 has always been high on my list of "next cars". When Wallace Wyss asked me to contribute photos for this book it was a welcome assignment. Over the years I have pointed my cameras at a great many 356s and the results have usually been good. I'd like to think this is due to my skills as a photographer but then again, with a subject like the 356, how can one miss.

Kurt Oblinger
Photographer and Historian
Redondo Beach, California

FOREWORD

I think the first time I ever saw a Porsche 356 was around 1952, when I was driving to Watkins Glen, New York, and I saw this funny looking little car parked by the road. Of course, I read the car magazines back then, including *Road & Track* and I knew what the hell it was—I just had never seen one.

It wasn't too long after that, around 1954, that I got to be a dealer, through "Maxie" Hoffman, the energetic Austrian who championed the Porsche, among other brands, and it was an odd little car to sell, because Americans who didn't know cars wondered how the hell we could charge $3,000 for something that was about half the weight of a Cadillac, but which sold for about the same price.

Of course, the Porsche customers read *Road & Track* too, and they knew what the car was, and that it was worth whatever we were charging for it. Though $3,000 in those days was a hell of a lot of money when you could buy a 2-bedroom house in Levittown for probably $10,000.

I was racing back then, in fact you could say I worked to finance my racing, and I leapt right around the road 356 models to the mid-engined Porsche race cars, the 550 spyder and RSK spyder. The only rear-engined 356 I raced was the Abarth Carrera GTL that I raced at Sebring in 1963 with Dan Gurney.

So except for customer's cars I drove back in the 1950s and early 1960s while I was servicing them, I can't tell you what it was like to drive 356s on the road.

But I can tell you that it was a great privilege to be one of the first to recognize the Porsche brand and what potential it had. Now, today, over 40 years later, Porsche is recognized throughout the world as a high-tech company. And our prices, to tell the truth, are still a lot higher than what Detroit sells cars for. But, dammit, the reason for that hasn't changed. We're trying to deliver what Detroit can't, or won't.

So I hope you have fun looking at Wally's book and looking back at the good old days with me. Those bathtub-shaped 356s were fun, though it was a bit odd back then being a champion of something so few people understood.

Bob Holbert
Holbert Motor Cars
1607 Easton Road
Warrington, PA 18976
October 1997

P.S. My son Larry, General Manager of our VW-Audi-Porsche dealership, has a collection of show condition 356 Porsches including a 1962 356 S90 Cabrio, a 1964 SC coupe, and a 1963 S90 coupe. Someday maybe he'll let me drive one of them.

ACKNOWLEDGEMENTS

The author would like to thank the following people for making this book possible:

Klaus Parr of the Porsche Factory Archive in Germany, for diligently searching the files for pictures that match those I found in old magazines.

The Porsche 356 Club Nederland in Holland has my gratitude for not only making their archive photos available but proofreading some of my book.

Special thanks to Jose Gochez III, of Jomart Intl., 356 Porsche restorer (1-800) JOMART 1 for his proofreading.

Special thanks as well to Bob Holbert of Holbert Motor Cars, 1607 Easton Road, Warrington, PA 18976

A debt of thanks to vintage racers, Abarth expert Dean Watts of Carson City, Nevada and Clint and Pat deWitt of Sacramento, California (who run DeWitt Motorsports), both of whom race pristine examples of 356 Porsches.

Thanks too, to Gary Emory of Porsche Parts Obsolete, 13851 S.E. Eola Village Rd. McMinnville, OR 97128.

The down-under contingent, Bob and Robyn Magowan of Auckland, NZ, are thanked for their input on right drive cars.

Additional thanks to Wayne Baker, Speedster owner, of San Diego, for his advice, and Chris Stabvoros, of San Diego, an expert in knock-off wheel 356s.

A 1949 Gmund-built 356/2. Note no chrome on rear 3/4 windows, low-mounted close-fit bumpers, "baby moon" wheel covers, split windshield with flat panes and low cut rear wheelwell.

INTRODUCTION

Following the end of the World War II, Austrian-born Dr. Ferdinand Porsche was detained by French authorities who were still miffed at his involvement in the design of wartime vehicles for the Third Reich (including the 56-ton Tiger tank). His son, Ferdinand (Ferry), was also detained briefly. Once released, Ferry moved back to their home country to start up a new business repairing farm vehicles. But he was intent on designing a new sports car and in getting a new business going by the time his father would be released. The small firm's first contract came from an Italian, Piero Dusio, and the result was a Grand Prix car called the Cisitalia. Unfortunately the project was underfunded, but the conception for the mid-engined car was brilliant.

Following that, Ferry thought maybe it was possible to create a sports car on a VW beetle chassis, using the same flat "Boxer" engine in the rear.

Two Swiss invested in their firm and in mid-1947 the firm rolled out its first car. That first Porsche was actually mid-engined, with the engine behind the driver and the gearbox behind the axle.

By the spring of 1948, the first production car was produced, using a 1131 cc engine rated at 40 hp, however, the production model had the engine behind the rear axle, like the VW beetle whose mechanical parts it used.

That first year, both coupes and convertibles were made, using aluminum bodies hand-hammered over hardwood formers.

In all, Porsche made 46 cars in Gmund, half of them open cars, before moving to Stuttgart. VW was offering to guarantee service of Porsche cars by VW agencies so a close bond was formed by the two automakers. When the Porsche team arrived in Stuttgart, they were also able to line up a body supplier, Reutter, who would make the coachwork in steel.

We can consider the hand-built Gmund cars all pre-production models, not series-produced cars. The series-produced 356s began production in Germany in 1950. They had the same basic shape as the Gmund cars, but already showed signs of evolution–the windscreens became wider and flatter, the roofs lower, the trim more plush.

Although the marque was only four years old, two alloy-bodied 1100 cc Porsches were entered at the 24 Hours of LeMans in 1951. One crashed in practice but the other finished 20th overall and 1st in class.

By 1951, the engine size was increased to 1300 cc.

By 1952, the 1500 cc engine was introduced in two versions, one with 55 hp, the other the Super with 70 hp In 1952 a special open model was developed for U.S. customers, fittingly called the America.

In 1953, they came up with an engine with the Hirth roller bearing crank. This robust engine would wind up to the incredibly high level of 5500 rpm, then considered a high water mark in rpm.

The Speedster went into full production in September 1954 (as a 1955 model) with the buyer's choice of 55 hp or 70 hp The Speedster was touted as a drive-to-the-racetrack-and-race model and the removable windscreen and lack of side window glass added to that impression. That model became famous in America because James Dean, the actor, raced one.

The interior of the Porsche was also evolving, especially the dashboard, which became progressively more modern as radio size decreased, and there was increased demand for instrumentation.

The "letter series" designations–A, B, and C–began in October, 1955 with the introduction of the 356-A. The body and chassis were redesigned, the wheels reduced in size from 16" to 15" and the dashboard changed.

In 1955, a model called the Carrera was introduced, using the same 4-cam engine design that had powered some of the Porsches that raced successfully in the Carrera Panamericana race through Central Mexico.

The ultimate Speedster was of course the Carrera Speedster, of which less than 200 were made.

In 1958, the Speedster was phased out in favor of a more civilized car with the same body but with roll-up windows and a taller windscreen–the Convertible D, the "D" standing for Drauz, the coachbuilder.

The "B" series came in the autumn of 1959. The headlights and bumpers were mounted higher. A new body style was introduced as well, the Roadster, a worthy successor to the Convertible D.

A short run model in the Bs (two years) was the Hardtop, made by Karmann, which looked like a roadster with a hardtop-style roof which was permanently attached.

In the meantime, Porsche's factory racing team was winning in sports car racing with their pure racing cars and 356 customers lived in hope that racing items would find their way onto the 356 option list, which they did quite often, such as in the case of the Carrera 4-cam engine.

And, of course, all over the world 356s were being raced by amateurs, in everything from rallies to races set up in America by marking out a course with haybales on the tarmac at Air Force bases.

One time Porsche pulled out all the stops and shipped a batch of 356-Bs to Italy for rebodying in aluminum by Carlo Abarth, Europe's recognized small car tuning genius. The resulting cars, called GT/Ls, were fast, and svelte, but not all German.

Back in Germany, Porsche continued to make a high performance Carrera model of the 356, still with mostly steel panels. In the B, this 4-cam was rated at 130 hp.

In the summer of 1963, the writing was on the wall–the 356's days were numbered. The final model made its debut–the 356-C. Mechanically, its big improvement was disc brakes all the way around. And the pushrod engine was up to 95 hp in the SC model. The Carrera model was carried over as well, though only 126 were sold. Design-wise, the 356 was by then looking rather "fat" compared to the leaner, sleeker cars being introduced by Porsche's rivals, yet demand continued unabated. Almost unnoticed was the fact that Porsche absorbed Reutter, their largest volume coachbuilder, so that at last Porsches were entirely built by Porsche, the chassis-body *and* the engine.

The biggest threat to the 356's existence was not a rival car made by another automaker but a rival made by Porsche themselves–the sleeker 911 model, with two more cylinders. It had started production in the summer of 1964 as a 1965 model. The 356 was living on borrowed time only because Porsche was having teething problems with the new flat six engine, and needed something to sell while they debugged the 911.

Finally the 911 was sorted out and Porsche realized that it no longer made sense to continue the old model while launching its replacement. 356 production shut down in 1965. A sop thrown to the four cylinder fans was the fitting of a four-cylinder 356 1600SC motor into a 911 body, sold as the 912.

But the 356 fans were having none of it. For them, the 912 was no substitute for their beloved "bathtub Porsche." For them, an era had ended. A total of 76,302 356s had been built over a 17-year period, many thousands more than the firm's founders had thought they would build at the beginning.

Usually in the car world, it is a couple of decades before collectors recognize a car's collectability and begin looking for older specimens and restoring them, but almost immediately after the 356 ceased production, collectors realized that it was time to start saving what had been wrought in the previous 17 years. What inspired them is the cars you see pictured here. Look through this book and I'm confident that you will agree that, individually and collectively, they represent a legacy worth saving.

Wallace A. Wyss
Riverside, California
June, 1997

Squint and you can see the basic shape of the 356 in this prewar design. At least three of these racers were built by Porsche in 1938 on VW beetle chassis as he developed a car for the Berlin-Rome race. His testers reached a high of 90 mph in testing but the cars were never run in the event, which was canceled because of the war. The streamliners never carried the Porsche lettering on the front originally—that lettering was added later by some misguided soul attempting to link the prewar design with the postwar Porsches.

Porsche No 1, May, 1948. There was much more flatness about this first design than the car that was mass produced, particularly in the line across the top of the body.

Porsche No 1 in "modern days" at the Monterey Historic. Somehow the beautiful art deco hubcaps disappeared and regular "baby moons" were installed, probably because those early tire sizes are impossible to find, and Porsche likes to keep their museum cars fully operational so they can make appearances.

Porsche No 1. The proportioning is remarkably like the mid-engined Boxster of 39 years later. The slots along the rear deck lid are tiny heat vent slots. The steering wheel is the "banjo" style popular on English cars. The windshield appears to have no frame other than the center support. The "A" on the rear flank designates country of registration (Austria) and the license plate indicates it was registered as a road car in the town of Karlsruhe.

The first Porsche had a Boxer (opposed piston) engine displacing 1131 cc with a bore of 75 mm and a stroke of 64 mm. It had a low compression ratio of 7:1 and was rated at 35 hp at 4000 rpm. The mid-mounted layout would have been better for weight distribution but for some reason Porsche decided to move the engine to the rear in the production version.

In 1948, a production "Gmund" coupe and the first roadster out on an Austrian road. Porsche 356s were assembled in Austria for only two years before the whole operation was moved lock, stock and barrel to Stuttgart. One reason was fear that if the new cold war turned hot a valuable firm would be lost to the Eastern sector.

Another view of a 356/2, the factory identifying this as the first coupe. The front trunk lid was very narrow at this time, probably because they thought making it too wide would compromise body rigidity. Later, they gained confidence in their car's strength and widened it.

A Gmund coupe being built in Austria, in 1948. Some say this was the first coupe built. The bumperettes indicate a willingness to add bumper protection but their thinness shows a resistance to adding weight.

A 356/2 Cabriolet interior. The seats, from Borgward, seem too plush for a sports car. Maybe at this stage Porsche was thinking of going for the luxury boulevardier market, but Porsche owners soon convinced them they were willing to go more spartan as long as it made the car fast. A Viennese firm, Keibl, built some of these early bodies.

The 1949 356/2 Geneva Salon car, bodied by Beutler in Thun, Switzerland on a chassis built in Gmund. License plate indicates Swiss registration.

Significant deviations from the style set by Porsche include bulging rear fenders reminiscent of the later Karmann Ghia, "art deco" full disc wheel covers, and a very long rear deck lid grate that does not attempt to follow the curve of the rear deck lid very much, as later became the practice.

A 1949 Gmund-built Porsche, still with the split windshield, but now a bit more brightwork, actually polished aluminum strips instead of chrome. Others made at the same time sometimes had the two front strips interrupted by a rectangular license plate frame.

Stuttgart, 1951. Unlike Detroit, where cars were hauled by mechanized conveyor belts, in Stuttgart, the 356s were hand pushed on dollies. A car did not move on to the next station until the work was completed. Shown here is an early cabriolet. Compared to the Gmund cars, the first Stuttgart cars had wider and flatter windscreens, lower rooflines, and lacked the shiny strips of metal between the directional signals.

Early on, car enthusiasts realized that air cooling meant you could take a Porsche almost anywhere and not worry about overheating. Hence the presence of this 1949 356/1 Gmund in Cairo. Porsche says it was the property of Prince Abd El-Moneim. Vertical slots on front fenders are trafficators—flip-out turn signal stalks also found on early VW beetles.

An American VW importer, Johnny Von Neumann, cut the roof off one of the alloy LeMans coupes to reduce weight and wind resistance. Here is the Von Neumann special owned and driven by Chuck Forge more than three decades later at the Monterey Historic. *Kurtis Oblinger.*

Dr. Ferdinand Porsche made his name with the Mercedes "S" racing cars in the 1920s. So it was natural that soon after his firm began production of his 356s there would be Porsches fielded in racing. This is a 1951 at LeMans, an all-alloy car, including front wheel spats to match those in the rear. The wire mesh headlamp lens protectors cut down on light emitted, but protected the lenses in a long race. Later, cast headlight grilles would be available.

In 1953, a Gmund-built coupe, a 356/2, follows a Borgward onto the starting line on a hillclimb at Freiburg, Germany. Unusual metal housing above the plate appears to be combination license plate light and turn signals. Door handles are still the blade-thin "switchblade type."

Another rally car, obviously with some sponsorship by the candymaker. This Austrian-registered car is competing in the 1954 Monte Carlo rally but the split windshield means it's an earlier car, perhaps a 1950 to mid-1952. Chrome headlamp shrouds were a factory option.

A 1950 pre-A coupe. This one still has the rear 3/4 windows, windscreen frame and rear backlight unadorned with brightwork. The hubcaps inexplicably have a black circle inscribed in them, more like those on a VW beetle, though the VW hubcaps had an interlocked "V" and "W" within the circle.

Stuttgart, 1951. With typical Germanic penchant for order, early on Porsche tried to make the cars all uniform in detail. But how do you explain the fact that the first car in line here has an air intake the others don't? They didn't succeed at getting them all alike until the "A" series started.

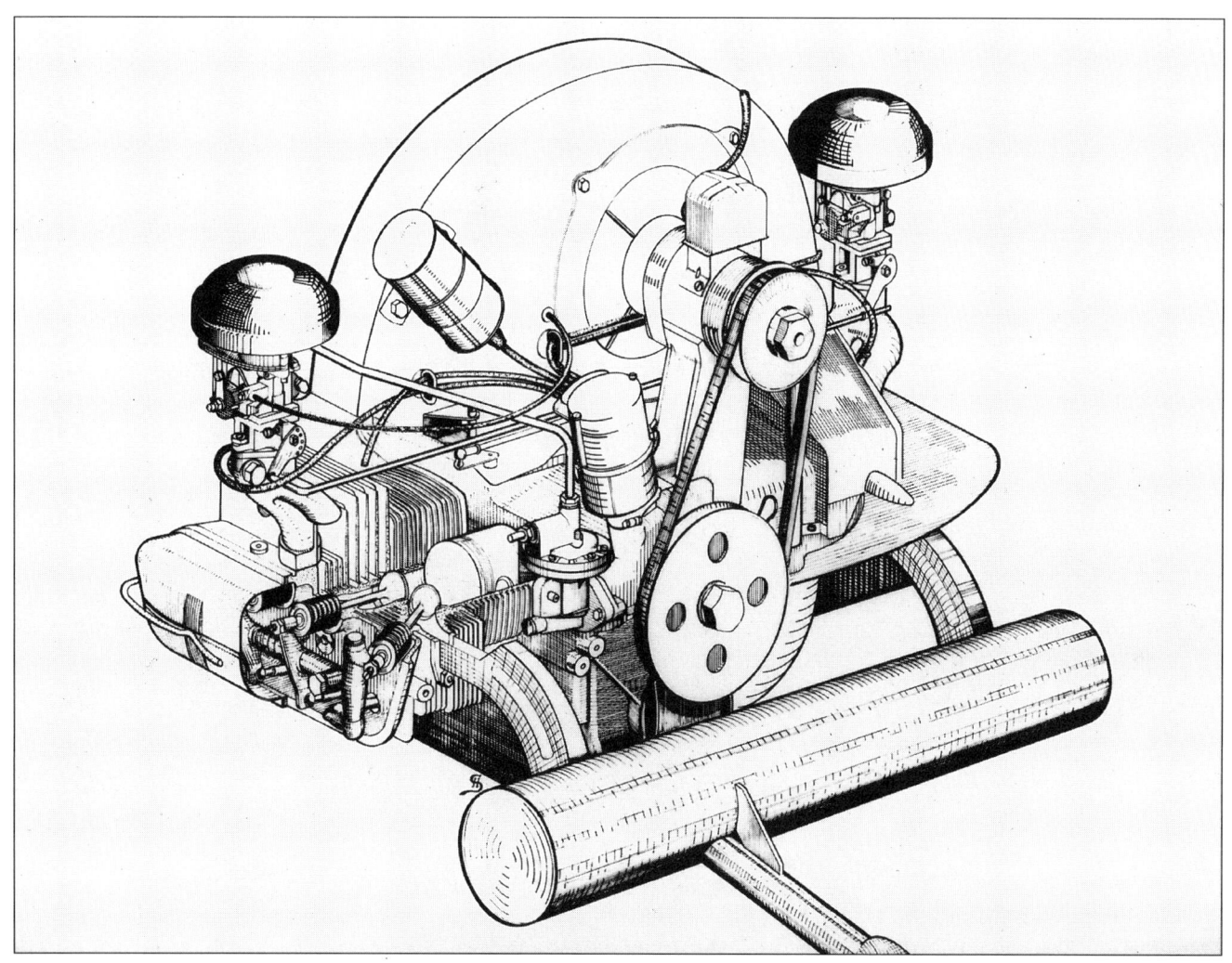

The early Porsche engines were really built up from some VW parts, including the VW engine, case, crankshaft, rods and carburetor. This was an early one, circa 1950, showing the dual Solex 32 PBI carburetors with the VW mushroom-shaped air filter covers. It was rated at 40 hp, quite a jump from the VW's 25 hp Porsche made a number of them with 1086 cc displacement in order to qualify them for the under-1100 cc racing class.

The 1950 Paris Auto Salon. The roadster was called the "Windhund" (windhound) a pet name for Ferry Porsche's own car. This picture is a clue to how small a company Porsche was at that time—the company's boss having to offer his own car for display. The windhund was later destroyed in testing.

Two pre-As line up for a race at Wilmont Hills, a Midwestern track, on October 3, 1954. Behind them is an MG-TF and–shades of *Herbie*–a VW Beetle. Note how Porsche on the left has "turbo trim rings."

Wilmont Hills, a Midwestern track, May 23, 1954. Considering this was the Heartland of America, there's a one heckuva lot of Porsches in this event. Porsche fans refer to these as "bent window" cars because, although Porsche had dropped the center split by then, the one-piece windshield came to a vee as if the split were still there...

This 1951 coupe has the slotted "turbo-discs" on 16" wheels that, thankfully, were short-lived on Porsches. Rear 3/4 windows were prop-opens.

An early car, most likely a 1951 with a Reutter body, and square Hella taillamps, is taken through a rally route. Porsche owners were willing to try almost any kind of speed contest, from land speed records to neighborhood rallies.

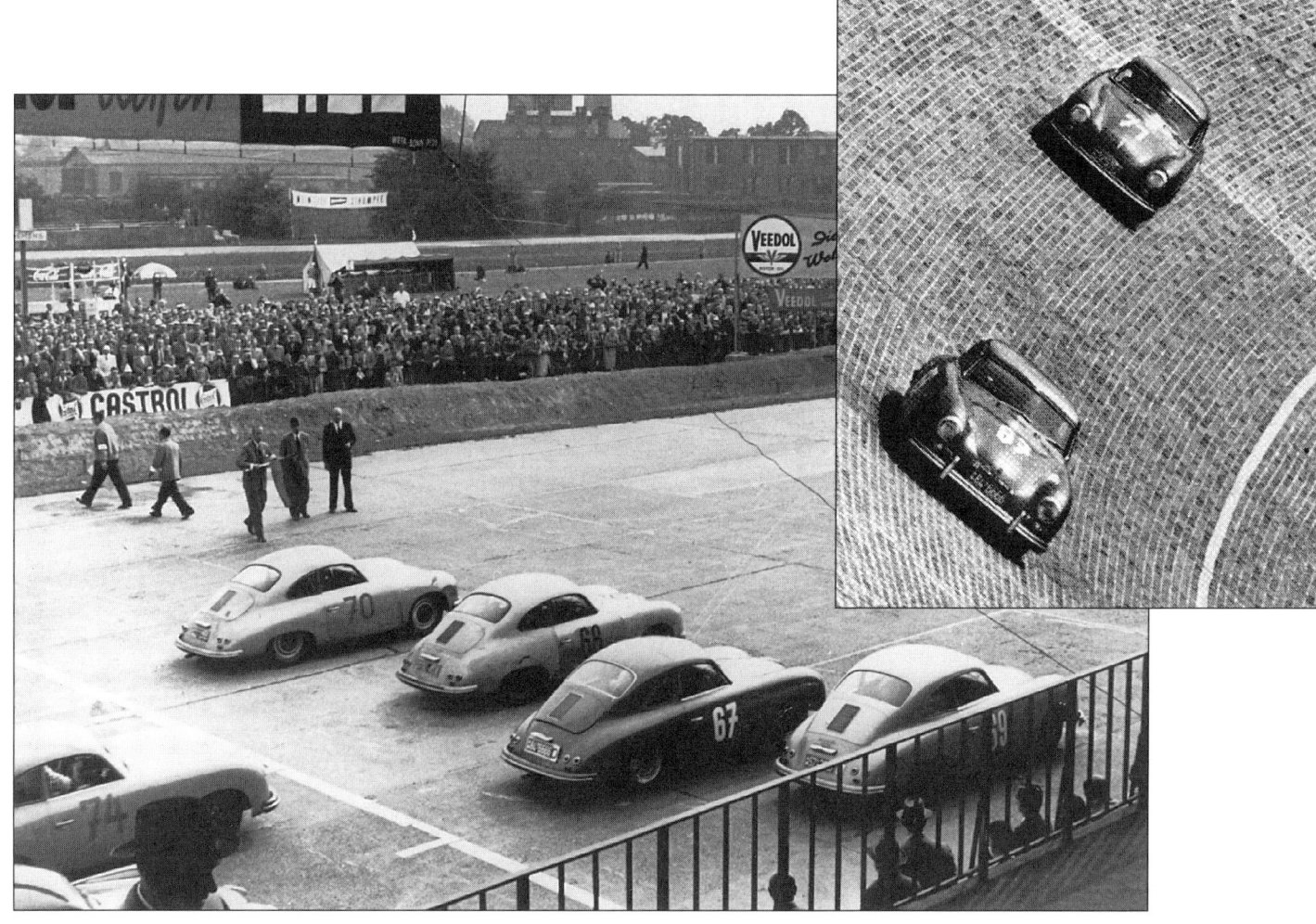

Avus was a famous German track, known for its banked section (inset). It was the "home track" for many German drivers. Here, in a 1955 race, two famous "bluebloods" are driving, Count Wolfgang "Taffy" von Trips in car #68 and Count Huschke Von Hanstein in car #67, who later became Porsche's personable PR man.

While the Mille Miglia is often thought of as the premiere event for Italian cars, the Germans frequently traveled over the Alps to enter, hoping to rob a class win in the under 2-liter classes. This is at the 1957 event, where the 356-A looks nearly stock except for the lack of bumpers. The year 1957 marked the last year of that event.

One of the best ways—and the least risky—to get attention to your new car was to attempt to set a record time on a closed course. This is a Type 356/2 attempting a record run at Montlhery in France, in 1951. Despite the fact Porsches were in production in Stuttgart, Porsche fell back on an alloy-bodied Gmund-built 356 for their record breaker. It was called a 356SL for "Super Light." Note front wheel spats like LeMans cars. The car also ran partial belly pans (as the Mercedes 300SL offered on the production gullwings.)

A fleet of 1952 "body-bumper" cars (so-called by American 356 fans because bumpers were attached right to the body, not free standing) prepares to leave the factory in Stuttgart-Zuffenhausen. One suspects this is a ride-'n-drive for journalists. These are bent windscreen cars. Note no uniformity to road lamp styles, some cars having rectangular lamps, others round ones.

The Porsche factory saw the Carrera Pan-Americana races in Mexico as a great opportunity to gain attention for their new models. This was down Mexico way in 1952 with a driver named Burchheim on the left and Prince Metternich on the right. The cabrio looks relatively stock, except the bumpers have been removed. One wonders if they raced in such casual dress, or if this shot was taken during a reconnaissance run?

Another race; this one a famous European rally—the Leige-Rome-Leige rally of 1952. Note how the drivers have taped over the fog lamps to prevent breakage before the night stages. Note how radio aerial goes up the center of the split windscreen.

A non-factory 356, but a very influential one. The one-off Sauter roadster was built in steel on a 356 chassis for a private German customer, Heinrich Sauter, with coachwork by a man named Klenk. Note how doors are hinged at the rear. The air intakes below the headlights were later picked up by Porsche for the 356. This is a Kurt Oblinger shot from the Monterey Historic, where Porsche was a featured marque in the late 1980s.

The dashboard of the Sauter roadster looks almost like a production Gmund dashboard even with such amenities as a glove compartment. But this is the car as photographed some 30 years after its inception, so one cannot be sure how much was changed by subsequent owners.

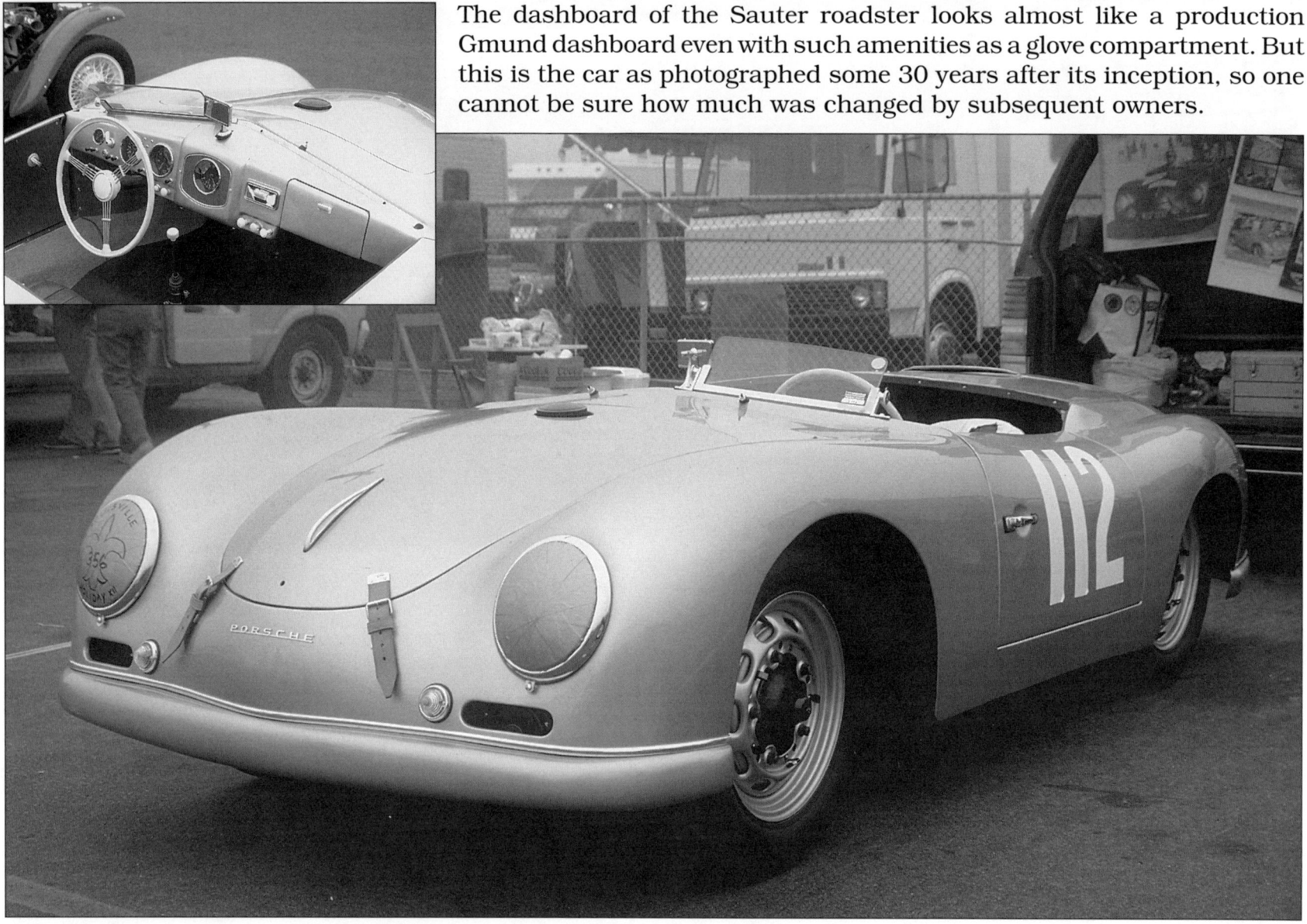

Kurt Oblinger captured the Sauter roadster in the pits at Monterey. Herr Sauter earned his place in history by influencing what the Porsche factory should build. The Sauter led to the America and the America to the Speedster.

An America being raced in America, where importer Max Hoffman saw great potential for the marque. This is Jack McAfee at Moffett Field, an Army-Air Force base in San Jose, CA. In the early days of sports car racing in America, race courses were often impromptu courses marked out by hay bales on airstrips.

Porsche bought the Sauter roadster in 1952, and copied the design for their short-lived Type 540 America model. They made only a couple of significant changes in adapting the design, including putting two vents on the rear decklid instead of one (after first running only one and finding that inadequate), and changing from rear-hinged doors to front-hinged ones (less embarrassment for the ladies, they say.) Coachwork started out in aluminum, ended up in steel in the final cars.

The America roadster interior had very plush looking bucket seats that were more along the lines of what you would expect in a Jaguar XK-120. There was even a clock on the instrument panel and hollow doors to store your oddments.

Pre-A 356. First clue is round "beehive" taillamps instead of teardrop-shaped ones. License plate and back-up light housing above bumper means pre-mid-1957 as, after that, the license plate light housing was moved below the plate.

This rare photo from the Archives of the Porsche 356 Club Nederland shows a Porsche America roadster parked with other just completed Porsches in 1952. In the early days the America's windscreen could be detached, but in the final models, the windscreen was molded in.

When Porsche described their engine as a "boxer" they meant that the pistons were opposing each other. The layout is seen here. The vertical lines are cooling fins cast into the outer skin of the air-cooled cylinder cases. Atop that—under the stamped metal covers—are the valves and rocker arm assembly. Below the center of the engine is the oil reservoir. This is a 1.5 liter 1500 Super which came in two states of tune.

Another period race shot from the Leige-Rome-Leige rally (1952 event) shows the "in" way to set up your road lamps, facing outward so they light up the corners. But these drivers apparently didn't feel it necessary to protect their headlamps until the night stages, counting on the factory die-cast headlight grilles to do the job.

The French Riviera is as good a place as any to have a rally, and who cares if you win—as long as you can attend the parties afterwards? This set of four pre-A 356s look to be all alike until you look closely and realize the car at left is the only one without curved-at-the-ends windscreen panes. It is obviously a full-skirted all-aluminum 356SL (Super-Light), a few of which were made for racing, adapted from Gmund-built alloy cars.

Stuttgart, 1953. Type 356s being hand-sanded, prior to being put into the drying booth. These are obviously pre-A's as seen by the four separate taillamps.

A mid-1952 dash. Among the items of interest are exceedingly comfortable looking seats, a two-spoke VDM steering wheel instead of the more common three spoke, a 200 km/h speedometer, a 6000 rpm tach and a one-piece windscreen free of the center "bar" at last. Note vertical push-button radio.

A production car race in 1953 at the "Ring" (nickname for the 18-mile long Nurburgring race course located in the Eifel mountains of Germany). Only one participant in this photo took the precaution to tape up his headlamps. At the 'Ring' and other tracks, it was also possible for civilians to pay a fee on non-race days and drive their own car around the track.

One purpose of racing was to call attention to the marque. For those who didn't go to race-tracks, the way to still make that connection was to bring the race cars right from the track to the car shows, sometimes with the dirt still on them. Here, at the 1953 Paris Salon, Porsche used a 550 Spyder as the crowd draw, hoping of course to sell the showgoers either the coupe or cabriolet on display.

From the beginning, Porsche dealers tried to get race cars to use as "people magnets", and this picture from a Freiburg, Germany showroom of 1954 shows a rare 550/4 spyder on display next to a production coupe. The race car was nicknamed the "Buckelwagen", it made its debut at the Brussels salon of January, 1954.

This is a very early car—a 1950, 1951 or 1952—as evidenced by the flat-paned windscreens that don't curve at the ends. Porsches were recognized early on as ideal for rallies, and this one is competing in the Monte Carlo rally. This driver runs both rectangular and the round auxiliary lamps, probably one set for fog and the other for long distance.

A pre-A model, with thin bumper guards, slight peak to roof despite one-piece windscreen. This could be a 1954.

Similar view of a 356-A, introduced in September, 1955. This shows how the bumper now stood out about 2" from the body. The "peak" of the roof has disappeared. Hood handle was made wider to accommodate Porsche crest.

A 1956 356-A, made more interesting because of its Carrera badging, which meant it boasted a 4-overhead cam engine like those used in the factory race 550s which won success in the Carrera Panamericana in Mexico.

The Carrera engine as seen in the 1954 550 Spyder "Buckelwagen."

The late 1950s models were so identical from year to year, that it is difficult to ascertain model years without seeing the car in person. Porsche enthusiasts tell this era apart by where the door latches were—1956-1957 1/2s having high strike door latches and the 1957 1/2 through 1959 the low-strike. This is a 356-A.

Another view of a 356-A Carrera coupe. If the "Carrera" nameplates on the fender and rear body didn't clue you in to the car's special nature, then maybe the two big bore exhausts and potent exhaust sound would. This is a pre-1957 1/2 model because it still has the "beehive" taillights.

A good view of a 356-A. In the As, the hood handle was wider at the bottom than the pre-As, so as to accommodate the factory's crest. Horns can be seen behind horn grilles which also contain housings for turn signal lenses.

This 1980s Kurt Oblinger shot catches an American racer who, in setting up his vintage racer, copied some of Porsche factory's racing mods for his vintage racing Porsche. In American historic racing, body modifications to a car are permitted if it can be documented that the factory also did those modifications at some point in the same models in the car's original era.

A Porsche factory archive photograph shows a factory-modified Porsche being used in a record-setting attempt at Monza. Among the mods—a "hard tonneau" around the driver and an aerodynamic headrest. By this time the factory had abandoned the wheel "spats" front and rear—probably because they slowed down tire changing time in the pits.

A Cabriolet, as evidenced by the vent windows, and permanently attached windshield frame. Teardrop taillights mean 1957 1/2 or later. Cabriolet body style gave much more headroom than the Speedster.

Jawohl, there were sunroofs available from the factory. One model was the Golde, with aluminum edging, and a hand-operated latch system. This shows one installed on a 356-A. Also visible through the side window are the "Sisal" floor mats—a rough-hewn plant-derived material with the texture of woven rope. It was designed to shake the dirt off your boots, more popular in Germany than America.

The DeWitts of Northern California vintage-race this Porsche bearing the name Continental. Porsche briefly used the name until Ford Motor Company imposed its might and pointed out they already had a car in the works with that name. Porsche dropped it. Bentley never complained though they had been using the name "Continental" since the early 1950s.

A tale of two interiors. The 356-A (above) has thicker seat backs and cloth inserts in the seats. Corduroy inserts started in 1953 and continued through 1965. A full leather interior (left) in a 356-A. Both seats shown have a spring-loaded hinge on the side of the seat back. Later seats had thinner steel-framed backs.

A Tale of two Speedsters. This view shows overrider tubes that most Americans prefer to run without.

The wrap-around of the Speedster's windscreen can be appreciated here. This is a rare Carrera model. There was also an even more rare Speedster Carrera GT with louvers on each side of the rear deck lid grille. This car has "split" rear overrider tubes.

If the man at left looks dour, it is explained by the fact that he designed and engineered the 356 from the beginning, and can always think of an improvement. He is Ferry Porsche. The man at the right is Ferdinand Alexander "Butzi" Porsche III, his son. The trunk lid on this 356-A Carrera stays up because it is counterbalanced. The "D" on the deck lid denotes German registration.

A second series Speedster interior, as exemplified by three equal size gauges. The ventilation slots cut into the wrap-around bucket seats were also a feature of many of Abarth racers in Italy. Porsche called their version a GT seat. Some had aluminum shells. Speedsters had no side windows, only plastic side curtains.

Rare, rare, rare—a 1957 Speedster with two rare options — wire wheels by Dayton and a hardtop, the top apparently having not only vent windows but fixed-in-place glass or plexiglass.

The Speedster was marketed as an almost ready-to-race car; hence no glove compartment, no provision for a radio (you had to sling it under the dash). This seat has piping, which could be ordered to match the exterior paint.

Vintage racing Speedster in America, at a Concours d'elegance. Wheels appear to be steel centers with polished alloy rims. Note "nerf" bars replacing factory bumpers, the chrome plated roll bar projecting beyond windscreen height and the non-Porsche "Talbot " mirrors.

A Speedster at the most basic of speed contests—a parking lot slalom (autocross). This one has non-period wheels and a full roll cage in addition to the roll bar. Makeshift spoiler and virtually flat windscreen aid aerodynamics, even at slalom speeds.

Did you ever see a more sanitary race course? It's the Tustin Thunder road races in Santa Ana, California. The Speedster has the tallest nerf bars in recorded history with road lamps attached to the nerf bars. A cute "period" touch is the British style spun-aluminum racing mirrors—definitely a 1950s item.

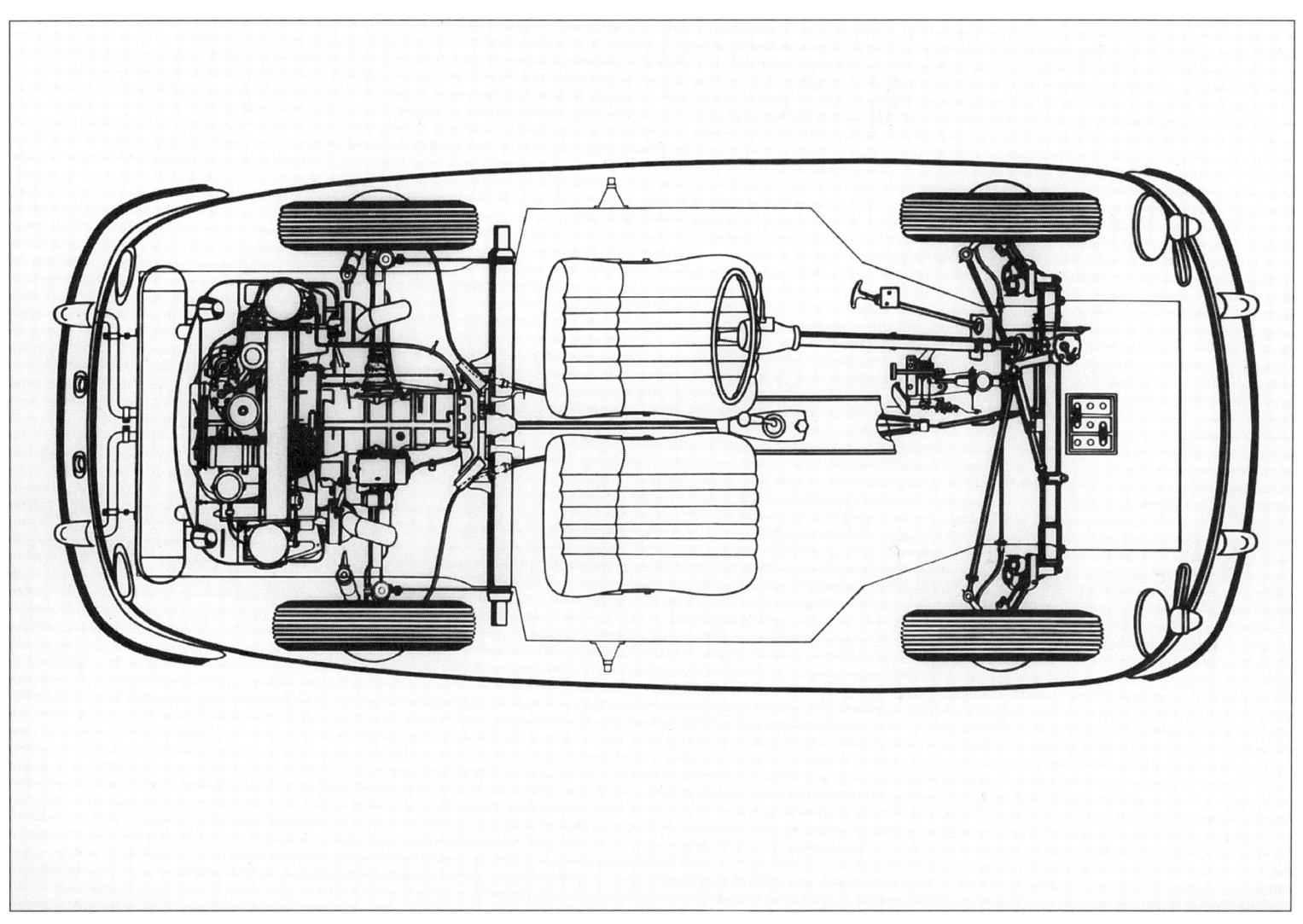

The layout of the 356 can be appreciated in this drawing of a 1962 356-B. The tires look ridiculously narrow by today's standards. Reminds you of the historic racer's line: "Remember when the tires were skinny and the drivers were fat...?"

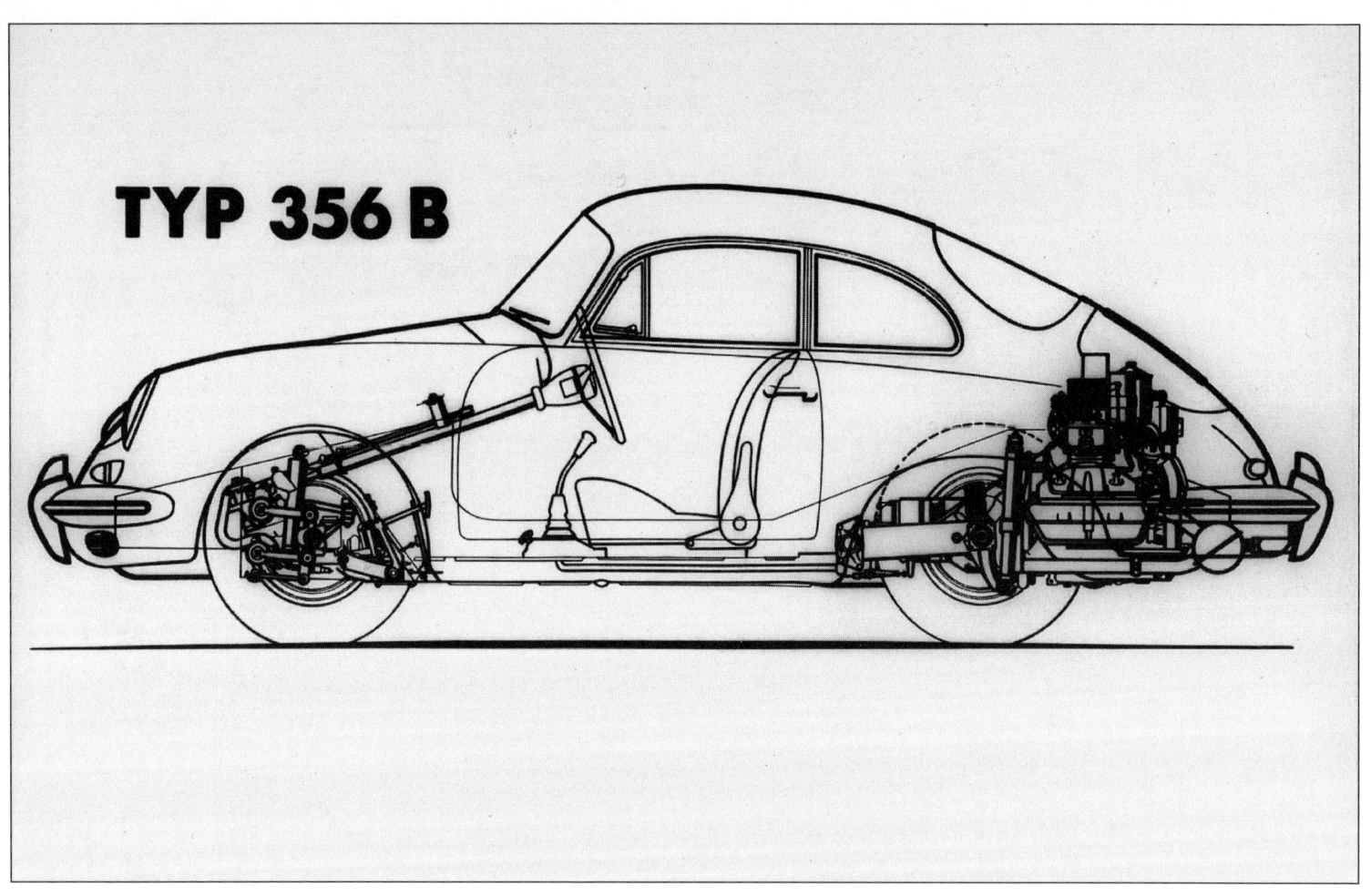

From the side view, there doesn't appear to be so much empty space. The Porsche body was as big as it needed to be and no bigger—unlike American cars of the Fifties where length and weight were what sold the car. ("A big car holds the road, yadda-yadda...")

Even the factory can slip-up—here is a shot from August, 1958 that shows a Convertible D still labeled as a Speedster with a big "D" on the chrome strip to designate "Drauz", the coachbuilder. The factory's last minute indecisiveness on naming reveals how reluctant they were to part with the "Speedster" name and model. Some experts claim that a few Convertible D's slipped out the door with this badging.

A 356-A cabriolet with two rare features—one it's a cabriolet with a Carrera engine, and two, it's got a hardtop.

A 1958 356-A Cabriolet with the rare Carrera option. Metal rocker strip has rubber inserted into it. Boot material on cabrios usually matched top material.

The Carrera engine in the Carrera 2 from 1962. Carrera engines were developed in 1953, and offered experimentally in at least 18 cars prior to being "officially" available in the 356-A. Eventually 4-cams were offered in all manner of body styles. By 1962, it displaced 1966 cc and was rated at 130 hp at 6,200 rpm. An annoying feature was eight spark plugs. The joke at the time was that, when the engine was hot, you had to be an asbestos octopus in order to change them!

A pushrod engine, probably from a "B"-as can be guessed by the single grille on the decklid. The gold-plated number on the car's rear deck identifies it as a 1600. The proper Porsche restorer makes sure everything not only has the original finish—which means resisting the temptation to chrome something that was not chromed originally, but also that some parts have proper—and properly placed—decals. Any mistake can lose you points in a concours!

A 1960 356-B coupe. This one exemplifies the changes from the "A" to the "B" series, which included a higher bumper design, a wider hood handle, and a redesign of the air intake grilles above the front bumpers. This is a drum-braked car, with raised-center crested hubcaps.

The fully accoutered Porsche 356 owner has sisal floor mats. This is a 1963 356-B Carrera, tipped off by the 250 km/h speedometer and a tach redlined at 7000 rpm. Note corduroy seats—Europeans liked cloth seat surfaces.

Did you ever see so many nuts holding on an air cleaner lid? This is a Super 90 engine with Solex 40 PII-4 carburetors. Porsche wanted to discourage you from taking off the air cleaners. Once the carbs ingested foreign matter, you lunched your engine, as this author can attest.

The special ducting in a 1958 Carrera GT shows "cold air box" on each side leading from the deck lid louvers right to the carburetors. The GT is among the rarest of Carrera models. Note single exhaust. This Reutter-bodied one dates to 1958.

The 356-B Karmann coupe. Don't be fooled into thinking they created this by just taking an open 356 and welding a hardtop in place. The rear 3/4 windows were actually larger than those available on the factory lift-off hardtop and were hinged so you could prop them open at the rear.

So rare that they are not even pictured in most Porsche books are the late 1950s GS/GT Carreras–identified by louvers on the rear decklid. GT versions were aimed toward racing, with everything done to reduce weight including going to plexiglass side windows, aluminum shells for the bucket seats and deleting the heaters. A roll bar was a factory option. Wheels had steel centers and aluminum rims and ugly non-shiny moon hubcaps. The GT fuel tank held 80 liters (21 gallons). Many of the GTs were sold as Speedsters, at least 48 of them in 1958 and 1959 inclusive. More luxurious was the GS or Grand Sport Carrera, also called Carrera de Luxe. Porsche identifies this cabriolet as a 1959 356-A Carrera 1500GS/GT.

One clue to a Carrera engine in a "B" model was removal of the horn grilles next to the turn signals. This was necessary because the horns were moved to be replaced by intakes for the oil cooler. Note nice fit of factory sunroof.

A popular style for those who missed the Speedster was the roadster. This is a famous picture from a Porsche calendar—and not a recommended way to travel to your favorite fishing hole.

Karmann bodies arrived from Karmann and were put into the mix of other models being built on the assembly line. Why did Porsche use so many coachbuilders? Because they often had more orders than any one coachbuilder could handle. Note how tight factory room was—cars were hand-pushed from one station to another.

A Karmann hardtop fresh from Karmann, ready for its wheels and mechanicals. Karmann also built some standard Porsche 356 bodies following the body styles of the previous coachbuilders.

A Karmann coupe being worked on at the factory. The movable tool tray was typical of the factory where the mechanics wheeled the cart around containing all their tools so they could fit the final few items and tune the car.

Cut a Porsche engine in half and it looks deceptively simple. This is a pushrod engine, as evidenced by the flat-topped fan housing. The fan belt was the key to the engine's longevity. If it snapped, you didn't go for long.

A cabrio at a concourse in California. How can you tell it's not a roadster? Roadster windshield posts had chrome trim and were removable while cabriolet windshield posts were part of the body. This is a 1962 or 1963 cabriolet, probably a 356-B with drum brakes because these hubcaps won't fit a "C". The back window was finally made zip-out in the cabrio by the time of the final version, body-coded T-6.

Porsche fans even get down to cataloging what accessories were available. This Porsche 356-B in ski country has a luggage rack (called "grid" in Europe) designed to tote skis. The racks had to be raised above the engine vent grate, lest the engine overheat.

The radio in this 1962 356-B is a Blaupunkt. It has three bands, one for short-wave. At that time Europeans liked to listen to short-wave broadcasts. The gauge above the radio in the car at the left is an instrument that wouldn't appear in American cars for decades—a gauge to show the outside temperature. The car above shows a right drive version sold in New Zealand.

The high point of the "Bs" was the 356-B Carrera GTL Abarth coupe—a car that came about when Porsche began to wonder if Carlo Abarth, the genius of small displacement Italian cars—could make a Porsche faster by rebodying it in his own inimitable style. Rather unsightly on this one are horn grates jammed into the front of the nose. The 21 Abarth GTL's all varied in details from one to another, Italians being less concerned with consistency from car-to-car than their German clients. Hole in body side was for quick access to torsion bars.

Perhaps to annoy the Germans, the Italians even fitted round taillamps on at least one of the Abarth 356s. This car has been fitted with a roll bar–a wise move. The bodywork was done by Zagato but the Zagato badge didn't go on them because Zagato didn't want to offend its other customers by bodying a foreign competitor. Auto company Abarth was the middleman.

Louvers? You like louvers? Abarth loved them. Additional fresh air was brought in by popping open a mini trunk lid. Bumpers were dispensed with—this was a race car that could be street driven. Taillights are from 356 parts bin.

On the interior Abarth used Porsche instruments with exception of a Smiths tachometer with a VDO face. They had the Abarth seats.

The dashboard of the Abarth shows the typical Italian penchant for whatever-is-not-important-is-not-there. Tach read to an impressive 10,000 rpm though the engine didn't quite get there.

It is rare to find a picture of an Abarth Carrera in its original unraced condition. This may be the first one built, as shown in Frankfurt, September 1959. The bodywork was by Zagato Carrozzeria, who bodied many of the racing Maseratis of the time, not to mention the Aston Martin DB4 GTZs. Writer Dirk-Michael Conradt attributes the styling to Franco Scaglione, who while at Bertone designed Alfa's B.A.T. prototypes and the production Alfa Sprint Speciale. This one has a black-lettered ABARTH lettering on the front flanks and the word PORSCHE spelled out in chrome on the hood. Other pictures show the Porsche crest worn on the hood of later cars.

Americans were sometimes faster in the factory race cars than Europeans. Here, at Sebring in 1962, Bob Holbert sits on the Abarth Porsche he drove. Another factory driver Edgar Barth, right, joins him for the picture.

A period shot of an Abarth GTL engine. Carburetors ran without air filters, but when parked were fitted with little carburetor stack covers, shown here.

A 356-A 1600GS engine, a direct descendent of the earlier 1500 Carrera engine designed by Dr. Ernst Fuhrmann. The Carrera engines had rounded fan housings. This engine is extremely valuable today. Unfortunately, when some owners of Carrera powered street cars experienced trouble in the 1950s, and found parts too expensive, they switched to a pushrod engine, greatly devaluing their original Carrera.

In case you were wondering what an aerodynamic race car would look like if Porsche themselves built one on a 356 chassis, here's what happened when the Germans had a go at it. It's called the 356-B 2000GS. Two were made on the GS/GT chassis with the 587/2 165 hp engine and with bodywork by DKS. While we can compliment the front (which looks suspiciously like a Matra D-Jet), the rear roofline is controversial, but at least predicted the forthcoming Ferrari 250LM (but without the sail panels.) Barth and Linge finished first in class and 4th overall in one at the 1963 1000KM in Germany.

The IAA in Frankfurt is the biggest new car show in the world. This is the 1963 show which shows a lot of access to the cars. One suspects this was the press preview period as there's too many guys in suits.

Porsche says this picture depicts a 356-B, but we say 356-C because the crested domed hubcaps of the "B" wouldn't fit the "C"; this car has the flat crested hubcaps of the "C".

A rare model—a 356-B cabriolet with the Carrera 2 option. The Carrera 2 option brought with it what you might call a "modesty" panel which covered up the unsightly Carrera exhaust, it not being possible to thread the exhaust pipes through the bumper guards because the holes wouldn't line up. Clue that this is a "B" is that these raised center crested hubcaps wouldn't fit a "C".

The best thing you could say about the 356 Cabriolet by the time it reached the "C" era was that the design was "optimized"—there wasn't a thing you could do to it without losing some of its unique character. Mirror on this one is a stainless steel Durant.

As the 356 neared the end of the trail with the 356-C, Porsche dropped the roadster so that if you wanted an open car, it was the Cabriolet or nothing. Note plain flat hubcap, the early ones having no crest.

This Carrera 2 has what are usually front bumper guards moved to the rear. It would have been silly to use the "holed" bumper guards because the Carrera exhaust wouldn't line up with the holes.

The final body style for the 356 came in 1962. The new design is the one on the right. It included two rear deck lid grates, a squaring-off of the front deck lid, moving of the gas cap to the top of the right front fender. Windscreen and rear backlight were enlarged on the coupe. So while it is easy to assume all the dual decklid large window models you see are "Cs", some are actually 356-Bs.

When the first 911 (originally called the 901 until Peugeot claimed they owned car names with an "0" in the middle) appeared, Porsche rolled it out next to a 356-C. Some early themes, Kurt Oblinger points out, were updated, like the horn grilles, and the exposed headlamps. But new things were added, like the huge front inset air intake on the 911.

From the rear, the 356 was definitely a dated car compared to its new sister car—having bulbous flanks compared to the slim trim 911. Porsche felt so guilty about dropping the four cylinder that they offered the 356 engine in the 911 body shell as the 912, thus making an entry level model so that the old owners could bridge the gap. But the 912 was never to sell in the same numbers as the 356s

The Iconografix Photo Archive Series includes:

AMERICAN CULTURE
AMERICAN SERVICE STATIONS 1935-1943	ISBN 1-882256-27-1
COCA-COLA: A HISTORY IN PHOTOGRAPHS 1930-1969	ISBN 1-882256-46-8
COCA-COLA: ITS VEHICLES IN PHOTOGRAPHS 1930-1969	ISBN 1-882256-47-6
PHILLIPS 66 1945-1954	ISBN 1-882256-42-5

AUTOMOTIVE
FERRARI PININFARINA 1952-1996	ISBN 1-882256-65-4
GT40	ISBN 1-882256-64-6
IMPERIAL 1955-1963	ISBN 1-882256-22-0
IMPERIAL 1964-1968	ISBN 1-882256-23-9
LE MANS 1950: THE BRIGGS CUNNINGHAM CAMPAIGN	ISBN 1-882256-21-2
LINCOLN MOTOR CARS 1920-1942	ISBN 1-882256-57-3
LINCOLN MOTOR CARS 1946-1960	ISBN 1-882256-58-1
MG 1945-1964	ISBN 1-882256-52-2
MG 1965-1980	ISBN 1-882256-53-0
PACKARD MOTOR CARS 1935-1942	ISBN 1-882256-44-1
PACKARD MOTOR CARS 1946-1958	ISBN 1-882256-45-X
SEBRING 12-HOUR RACE 1970	ISBN 1-882256-20-4
STUDEBAKER 1933-1942	ISBN 1-882256-24-7
STUDEBAKER 1946-1958	ISBN 1-882256-25-5
VANDERBILT CUP RACE 1936 & 1937	ISBN 1-882256-66-2

TRACTORS AND CONSTRUCTION EQUIPMENT
CASE TRACTORS 1912-1959	ISBN 1-882256-32-8
CATERPILLAR MILITARY TRACTORS VOLUME 1	ISBN 1-882256-16-6
CATERPILLAR MILITARY TRACTORS VOLUME 2	ISBN 1-882256-17-4
CATERPILLAR SIXTY	ISBN 1-882256-05-0
CLETRAC AND OLIVER CRAWLERS	ISBN 1-882256-43-3
ERIE SHOVEL	ISBN 1-882256-69-7
FARMALL CUB	ISBN 1-882256-71-9
FARMALL F-SERIES	ISBN 1-882256-02-6
FARMALL MODEL H	ISBN 1-882256-03-4
FARMALL MODEL M	ISBN 1-882256-15-8
FARMALL REGULAR	ISBN 1-882256-14-X
FARMALL SUPER SERIES	ISBN 1-882256-49-2
FORDSON 1917-1928	ISBN 1-882256-33-6
HART-PARR	ISBN 1-882256-08-5
HOLT TRACTORS	ISBN 1-882256-10-7
INTERNATIONAL TRACTRACTOR	ISBN 1-882256-48-4
INTERNATIONAL TD CRAWLERS 1933-1962	ISBN 1-882256-72-7
JOHN DEERE MODEL A	ISBN 1-882256-12-3
JOHN DEERE MODEL B	ISBN 1-882256-01-8
JOHN DEERE MODEL D	ISBN 1-882256-00-X
JOHN DEERE 30 SERIES	ISBN 1-882256-13-1
MINNEAPOLIS-MOLINE U-SERIES	ISBN 1-882256-07-7
OLIVER TRACTORS	ISBN 1-882256-09-3
RUSSELL GRADERS	ISBN 1-882256-11-5
TWIN CITY TRACTOR	ISBN 1-882256-06-9

RAILWAYS
CHICAGO, ST. PAUL, MINNEAPOLIS & OMAHA RAILWAY 1880-1940	ISBN 1-882256-67-0
CHICAGO&NORTH WESTERN RAILWAY 1975-1995	ISBN 1-882256-76-X
GREAT NORTHERN RAILWAY 1945-1970	ISBN 1-882256-56-5
MILWAUKEE ROAD 1850-1960	ISBN 1-882256-61-1
SOO LINE 1975-1992	ISBN 1-882256-68-9
WISCONSIN CENTRAL LIMITED 1987-1996	ISBN 1-882256-75-1
WISCONSIN CENTRAL RAILWAY 1871-1909	ISBN 1-882256-78-6

TRUCKS
BEVERAGE TRUCKS 1910-1975	ISBN 1-882256-60-3
BROCKWAY TRUCKS 1948-1961*	ISBN 1-882256-55-7
DODGE TRUCKS 1929-1947	ISBN 1-882256-36-0
DODGE TRUCKS 1948-1960	ISBN 1-882256-37-9
LOGGING TRUCKS 1915-1970	ISBN 1-882256-59-X
MACK® MODEL AB*	ISBN 1-882256-18-2
MACK AP SUPER-DUTY TRUCKS 1926-1938*	ISBN 1-882256-54-9
MACK MODEL B 1953-1966 VOLUME 1*	ISBN 1-882256-19-0
MACK MODEL B 1953-1966 VOLUME 2*	ISBN 1-882256-34-4
MACK EB-EC-ED-EE-EF-EG-DE 1936-1951*	ISBN 1-882256-29-8
MACK EH-EJ-EM-EQ-ER-ES 1936-1950*	ISBN 1-882256-39-5
MACK FC-FCSW-NW 1936-1947*	ISBN 1-882256-28-X
MACK FG-FH-FJ-FK-FN-FP-FT-FW 1937-1950*	ISBN 1-882256-35-2
MACK LF-LH-LJ-LM-LT 1940-1956 *	ISBN 1-882256-38-7
MACK MODEL B FIRE TRUCKS 1954-1966*	ISBN 1-882256-62-X
MACK MODEL CF FIRE TRUCKS 1967-1981*	ISBN 1-882256-63-8
STUDEBAKER TRUCKS 1927-1940	ISBN 1-882256-40-9
STUDEBAKER TRUCKS 1941-1964	ISBN 1-882256-41-7
WHITE TRUCKS 1900-1937	ISBN 1-882256-80-8

* This product is sold under license from Mack Trucks, Inc. All rights reserved.

The Iconografix Photo Gallery Series includes:

CATERPILLAR PHOTO GALLERY	ISBN 1-882256-70-0

The Iconografix Photo Album Series includes:

CADILLAC 1948-1964	ISBN 1-882256-83-2
CORVETTE PROTOTYPES & SHOW CARS	ISBN 1-882256-77-8
DODGE PICKUPS 1939-1978	ISBN 1-882256-82-4
LOLA RACE CARS 1962-1990	ISBN 1-882256-73-5
LOTUS RACE CARS 1961-1994	ISBN 1-882256-84-0
McLAREN RACE CARS 1965-1996	ISBN 1-882256-74-3
PORSCHE 356 1948-1965	ISBN 1-882256-85-9

All Iconografix books are available from direct mail specialty book dealers and bookstores worldwide, or can be ordered from the publisher. For book trade and distribution information or to add your name to our mailing list contact

Iconografix
PO Box 446
Hudson, Wisconsin, 54016

Telephone: (715) 381-9755
(800) 289-3504 (USA)
Fax: (715) 381-9756

MORE GREAT BOOKS FROM ICONOGRAFIX

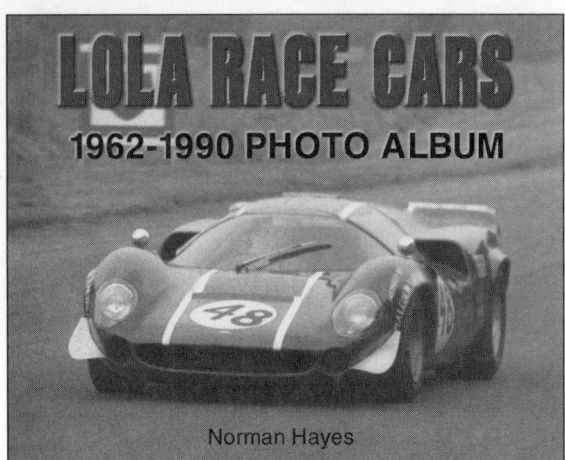

LOLA RACE CARS 1962-1990
Photo Album ISBN 1-882256-73-5

LOTUS RACE CARS 1961-1994
Photo Album ISBN 1-882256-84-0

LE MANS 1950: THE BRIGGS CUNNINGHAM CAMPAIGN
Photo Archive ISBN 1-882256-21-2

McLAREN RACE CARS 1965-1996
Photo Album ISBN 1-882256-74-3

FERRARI PININFARINA 1952-1996
Photo Album ISBN 1-882256-65-4

SEBRING 12-HOUR RACE 1970
Photo Archive ISBN 1-882256-20-4

VANDERBILT CUP RACE 1936 & 1937
Photo Album ISBN 1-882256-66-2

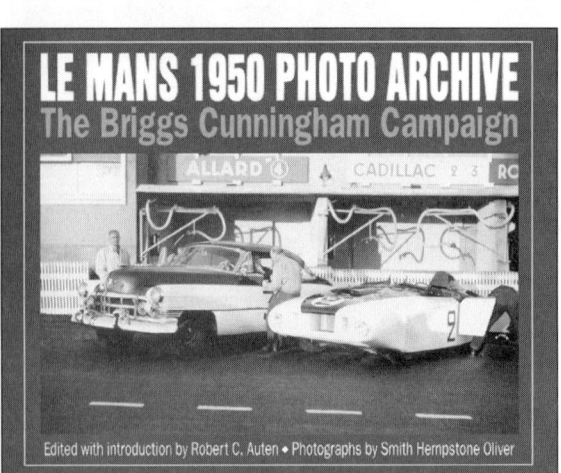

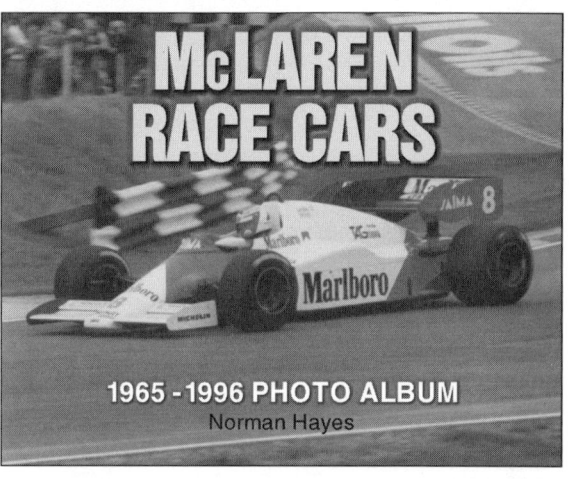